To Barry, with al

2023

# THE WORM
# IN THE APPLE

David Singleton

Grosvenor House
Publishing Limited

The right of David Singleton to be identified as the author of this
work has been asserted in accordance with Section 78
of the Copyright, Designs and Patents Act 1988

This book is published by
Grosvenor House Publishing Ltd
Link House
140 The Broadway, Tolworth, Surrey, KT6 7HT.
www.grosvenorhousepublishing.co.uk

A CIP record for this book
is available from the British Library

ISBN 978-1-78623-498-8

# INTRODUCTION

Just over two years ago, I was diagnosed with prostate cancer. The first part of this book describes the process of diagnosis and my subsequent treatment. It has been a period of some anxiety, but also of wry reflection on the absurdity of the human condition.

The second consists of the poems written during the two years since my diagnosis. I am surprised how numerous they are. Many are about cancer and its treatment; others are not.

This book is dedicated to the many friends, too many to name but not too many to love, who have helped me and to the staff of the Royal Bolton and Christie Hospitals who have cared for me over this last two years. Please accept it with my profound gratitude and love.

# CONTENTS

# OUR CANCER

# FINDING OUT

It was at a performance of Wagner's Ring that I first admitted to myself that things were not only far from well, but needed to be addressed. For years, I had suffered mildly from urinary tract infections. This was different.

Wagner, of course, is the severest test of the bladder in the operatic repertoire. The first act of Die Walkure contains some of Wagner's most passionate and lyrical music, but there is a great deal of it; in a phrase, it goes on. When, within ten minutes of the start, you become conscious of a burning sensation in the urethra, accompanied by a desperate desire to pee, the evening becomes a memorable one. By the time we arrived at "Du bist der Lenz," the unorthodox passions of Siegfried and Sieglinde had long ceased to matter to me. My world was focussed entirely on a circle of porcelain.

In the end, I got there, but I noticed a very faint tinge of blood in the urine: not for the first time, but the first time for some years. This alarmed me, but not enough. I put it down to having drunk white wine, which has often disagreed with me, despite my earnest efforts to come to a better understanding. I did nothing about it, and the problem seemed to go away.

Not for good. I was by now in my 70th year and not surprised that bits of me seemed to be working less well than previously. As I moved through the autumn of 2016, I therefore attributed to old age the fact that I needed to pee more often, to get up several times in the night and to be close to facilities during the day. It was increasingly irksome to urinate and still be left with the desire for more; it was worse, much worse, to need to urinate and be unable to do so. Visits to the loo in the small hours became increasingly prolonged and exhausting.

It was time to overcome a lifetime of reluctance, and go to the GP. It is strange phenomenon, this male aversion to seeking medical help: in my case, the main cause in my case is a mixture of vanity and embarrassment. I see the admission of physical weakness as a personal failure: a medical examination is, for me, an exam in the usual sense: not a neutral search for data, but a test of my value. I did not expect the results to be good. After several weeks of attempting to cajole a feeble stream of urine from my reluctant penis, I knew there was rather more to it than simply "getting old."

So, off I went, on one of those slate-grey days that usually precede Christmas. I wore a suit and tie, thinking that if I was going to be diagnosed with an old bloke's ailment, at least I didn't have to wear old bloke's clobber. I looked smart and I wore my best Hugo Boss underpants and washed my nether quarters three times, just to be on the safe side.

I hadn't met the GP before; this is quite usual in the group practice I attend. It appears to operate as as a rotational squad, like a premiership team. The Doctor was young, female and immediately inspired confidence. After a brief discussion of my symptoms, she concluded,

"Clearly an enlarged prostate. We need to check that that's all it is."

"How do we do that?"

"Two ways. An examination, which has to be rectal, and a blood test to check the PSA. These can be done in any order, but they must be done a week apart. Which would you like to do first?"

"Let's get the rectal examination over with. Can you do it now?"

"Yes, but first I am required to ask you if you would rather be examined by a man."

"Christ, no! Men have got thicker fingers."

"Do you require a chaperone?"

I replied that it was some decades, if ever, since the sight of my naked posterior had provoked ungovernable lust. I was prepared to take the risk. Sad to say, this rather witty reply of mine provoked nothing beyond a thin and wintry smile. It has been a disappointment of the whole process of my diagnosis and treatment that the Doctors do not laugh at my jokes; perhaps it is in the Hippocratic oath somewhere – or perhaps my jokes just aren't very funny.

So it came about that I found myself with my trousers around my ankles, knees raised to my chin, face to the wall of the surgery, with a young woman's two fingers firmly lodged in my fundament. I found it slightly reassuring that I gained no pleasure from the experience whatsoever.

"Yes," she said, after what felt like some hours of exploration, "I can't really get far enough in but it does feel a bit enlarged. Let's see what the blood tests say, but even if there's something sinister, there's heaps we can do."

I made the appointment, which had to be after Christmas, and waited – not, to be honest, with any great apprehension. I wasn't blasé about prostate cancer; I knew better than to regard it as a sort of rite of passage into old age. I was simply relieved: I had done my duty, and had handed over responsibility for my health to someone better able to care for it. I felt in that an enormous sense of release; I was no longer on my own. I was "in the system."

Christmas was mostly somnolent: Margaret and I went to our cottage in Cumbria and slept. I cannot recall being especially worried; on my return, I duly went for the appointed blood test – I think it was on a Friday. On the following Monday, something rather dramatic happened. We had then a ginger Persian cat, called Bertie. He was extremely loveable, but also extremely stupid. Several times a week, he dashed incontinently about the house howling, for no better reason than that he enjoyed running and making a noise. Unfortunately, many of the floors in the house are tiled. Bertie could not always stop himself in full flight, and often collided with doors, walls or furniture, always with a loud bang.

On this occasion, we heard the usual concussion from the hall and found Bertie momentarily unconscious and lying on his side twitching. We thought he might be having some kind of fit. So, we took him to an animal hospital some miles away where a charming Italian vet recommended a blood test (at a cost of £250). As she took the cat away, I said,

"Are you sure you don't want any help?"

"Why? He won't be naughty, will he?"

I reflected on the overwhelming probability that Bertie, now much restored, would indeed be "naughty." But in these circumstances I believe in leaving it to the professionals. The two of them, Bertie and the vet , disappeared into a surgery for some time, and finally emerged, Bertie with the light of battle in his eye, the vet looking slightly haggard.

"Ring up tomorrow for the results. No need to bring him back."

The second sentence was, I thought, given some emphasis.

And so, we went home. Almost immediately, the phone rang. It was the GP surgery ; one of the doctors came on.

"It's about your PSA score. 500."

"Is that good?"

"It's very high. With a score like that, there is almost certainly a little cancer in there somewhere. I'm going to send you to the Royal Bolton on the 14-day rule, but don't worry. This sort of thing is eminently treatable these days."

I wondered momentarily whether there might be a distinction between treatable and curable, but my first job was to tell my wife:

"It looks as though I've got prostate cancer."

"Oh," she wailed, "not two of my boys!" So I ranked alongside Bertie! I was pleased at this; I thought my status had been less elevated.

# DIAGNOSIS

There is something rather special about getting cancer, even the rather commonplace one to which I had been allocated. It gives you a certain status, even an aura, creates a kind of distance between you and the non-cancer suffering world. There is something a little ominous about it, even now; it must be rather like being a priest, or a vicar. There is something of "the other side" about you; you feel it yourself; others feel it in you.

People – friends, family – have to be told – or at least, I suppose they do. My instinct, as about most things, would have been to keep quiet about it, but Margaret wasn't having any of that, and indeed, I could not argue with her right to seek the support of her friends, as needed. I left most of the telling to her. The fact that you have cancer is a little difficult to slip into a conversation. You can, I suppose, always start off, breezily,

"Guess what? I've got cancer?"

But the conversation that follows tends to be on the stilted side:

"Where?"

"In Bolton."

"No you bloody fool. Which bit of your body."

"Oh, I see what you mean. The prostate."

People know about these things these days. Almost everyone can locate the prostate, at least approximately, as somewhere south of the bum, ideally located to cause trouble to the smooth operation of the waterworks. A few of my friends had slightly more specialized knowledge:

"What's the PSA score?"

"500."

A silence would ensue, though I fancy I heard a whisper of "oh shit!" at the end of one line. Everyone offered, more or less convincingly, an attempt at reassurance, except perhaps my sister, whose outlook on life has been modelled on the Book of Job.

"You seem very cheerful about it! Aren't you afraid?"

"What of?"

"Well…pain, suffering and death."

And that, of course, was just for starters. She omitted to mention the sufferings, no doubt considerable, that would doubtless await me in the afterlife.

On the whole, though, I was immensely heartened by the reaction of friends and friends of friends. The great majority expressed, not only sympathy and shock ("no, surely not you" was a strangely common reaction), but a willingness to help, with whatever assistance was needed. For the first time in my life, I felt vaguely popular.

I was therefore not in low spirits when I went to the Royal Bolton Hospital for the first of the consultations that led to formal diagnosis and a plan of treatment. Just as well, because it is not an institution calculated to raise the spirit. Older people in Bolton (older than me, that is, if there still are any) still refer to it as "Townleys," the name of the workhouse that was established there at the end of the nineteenth century, and grew over the decades into a large and sprawling hospital site. The original, rather Italianate, building is still there, surrounded by more modern buildings with no pretence at architectural distinction whatever. They are linked by endless corridors, painted for the most part a dyspeptic green, and there is no logic whatever in the siting of the constituent parts. Thus, urology, which was the focus of my visit, occurs in two places – at opposite ends of the hospital. To move from one site to another entails a walk of half a mile. It pays to be fit to visit RBH.

Which, of course, most people are not. It is impossible to stand near the main entrance of the hospital without being struck by how poorly people look. You might indeed expect this of the patients, but it seems almost equally true of the visitors: poorly dressed, poorly nourished, often obese, barely mobile, struggling for breath, faces pinched by exertion and worry. You are reminded at once that you are in Farnworth, which is one of the poorest parts of greater Manchester. The poor die earlier than the rich, and this is where they come to do it.

I have history with the RBH – or at last my in-laws do. Both my parents-in-law died there. Neither received the consistent quality of care we felt they deserved. My mother in law in particular, by then suffering from dementia, was allowed to fall unobserved. She never recovered from a broken hip and subsequent complications, despite an unconscionable and abortive attempt to discharge her into a care home. After her death, her daughters successfully pursued damages from the Trust.

I had therefore no great expectations of the RBH, though I approached my consultation with the confidence that springs from knowing that my bum could not have been cleaner and that my underpants were fresh on in the last hour.

The urology clinic was a delightful surprise. Firstly, the staff were friendly; we arrived early, and when I enquired if we could get a cup of coffee, a woman in a white uniform immediately made us one. The consultant was running a little late, but we were told courteously why:

"It's Mr Gkentzis today. He's not back from the wards. He's Greek. But don't worry. He's very nice."

My height and weight were checked, and I was asked to pee into a bottle. After all, it was a urology clinic. Analysis showed that I had a severe urinary tract infection, as well, apparently, as the cancer. This seemed to be gilding the lily somewhat, but such is the lot of the seventy-year old male. There do seem to be a lot of us about, however. The clinic was full of men about my age; I was easily the healthiest looking, and I dare say I had the cleanest bum and the newest boxer shorts.

Agapios Gkentzis fully lived up to his billing. He was Greek, and I much enjoyed the admirably accurate transliteration of his name: Genzis would have been unforgivably slovenly, and rather Turkish. He was young (though my standards in this area are slipping), engaging and professionally impressive. Greeks do not, however, tend to have small hands, and this was one area in which he might profitably seek improvement. The inevitable rectal examination was even less enjoyable than before. Moreover, he failed to comment on the surely unprecedented resplendent condition of an organ which surely, in Bolton, cannot always be so fragrant.

He was not short, however, of other commentary:

"Mmm, " he said, "feels a bit enlarged. With a PSA of 500 there's bound to be a cancer there. We need to do some tests to see if there's any spread, then a biopsy to check whether we need to offer you chemotherapy. But we can start some treatment now. As it happens, you have a pretty severe urinary tract infection, which we need to treat with antibiotics, as well as the tumour, which we can treat through starving it by denying it testosterone."

This was not entirely good news:

"So you're talking about chemical castration, in effect?"

"Not necessarily, and not for ever. You will almost certainly get hot flushes. You may grow breasts and there may be some erectile dysfunction."

"Oh, " I thought, "Is that all?"

"Are there any more side-effects?"

"Well...weight gain is hard to avoid, and there can be emotional effects." I assumed that by that he was not referring to uncontrolled euphoria.

"So ...it's just tablets, is it?"

"Tablets at first. Then a series of injections; but we can arrange this to fit in with any holiday plans you may have."

And so, I left, wondering whether to change my name to Teiresias, and clutching several boxes of NHS drugs. Farnworth is not the most enticing of areas. It has rarely looked bleaker than on that January afternoon.

The scans were duly conducted. I had a pelvic scan and a whole body scan; both involved, so far as I can remember, sitting in a large metal doughnut in a room from which the attendants fled as the scanner began working. It seemed absurdly undramatic for so potentially life-changing an event, but then, a slightly disappointing absence of drama has been characteristic of the whole process so far, perhaps because so much of it has been conducted in the presence of people for whom cancer is not only an everyday event, but the phenomenon that pays their mortgage. Life happens; then, it doesn't. It is useful to be reminded of that. I personally draw some comfort from the fact that all matter is indestructible. It is easy to forget, in Farnworth, that we are all made of atoms that came initially from a supernova. But it is true. Someone once told me that bush in my garden almost certainly contained an atom or two recycled from the mortal remains of Johann Sebastian Bach. I looked at that piece of vegetation with a new respect once I realized that it had in some small part contributed to the Well-tempered Clavier.

I then saw Mr. Gkentzis again, enthused by the prospect of the final biopsy. This is a further rectal examination, assisted by a

THE WORM IN THE APPLE

kind of periscope, followed by the chopping off of twelve small chunks from the tumour itself. It sounds somewhat invasive, and it is, and though not precisely painful, it is uncomfortable. It is like being penetrated by a baseball bat, with a circular can-opener at the end. But alas, it could not be done, or not yet. I still had, despite very powerful antibiotics, a UTI.

"Let's look at the scans," said the consultant, "no sign whatever of spread." This was good news, of course. "We can postpone the biopsy. When are you going to India? We can do the biopsy when you get back." This was even better news. We had a tour arranged, mainly of Rajasthan, for February with our dear friends, David and Patsy Hinchliffe. The tour was, in the event, as magical as we had hoped, and well worth the crushing disappointment of having to postpone further anal penetration for a whole two weeks. If there is a heaven, and if one has choice of precise venue, I should be happy to spend eternity in the garden of the Samode Haveli at Jaipur.

My biopsy was thus fixed for late February, when I found myself in the capable hands of Miss Lee (or perhaps more properly Miss Li); it might be more accurate to say that I found her capable hands in me. I was instantly encouraged by the sight of Miss Li. It was not just that she created an immediate impression of professional expertise, though she did. No; what was most impressive about her was that she was very small, with slender hands.

"Thank God, " I thought, "No more hefty masculine fingers."

Miss Li carefully explained what she was about to do to me – or, as she might prefer to have put it, for me. Rather to my surprise, she said that I might, as the cutting tool worked, feel a "slight crack." I had taken that to be her role. Then she continued:

"I have a request to make. You don't have to say yes." It is not, I suggest, easy to say no to someone who has the power to do immediate and unpredictable damage to the inner workings of your fundament. " I have a student. It would be very helpful if he could come and have a look, just to get his hand in, so to speak."

I feared the worst, but I had spent my entire life in education. I could not decently refuse an opportunity to a youthful seeker after enlightenment, even if the search was to be conducted in my intimate quarters.

"Do please feel free," I said with exquisite courtesy.

At that moment, the door swung open, and in walked a six feet five behemoth, with hands like clusters of bananas and fingers grown muscular and calloused from the clutching of rugby balls.

"This," said Miss Li, "Is James."

"Very nice, " I think I replied, from somewhere near the bottom of the Slough of Despond. At last I know how Betjeman felt (though Bunyan may have been there before him). Life had pulled another of its scurvy little tricks.

So, they probed away in tandem, though not at the same time.

"Oh, come and look at this James. It's only on one side. It doesn't look that abnormal."

But actually, it was.

I have read recently that there is a move to replace the prostate biopsy with a MRI scan. If that can be done, it should be. The biopsy is uncomfortable, moderately humiliating and invasive. It is not without its dangers. In my case, it engendered an infection which was to plague me throughout my treatment.

The north-west of England is a very good place to have prostate cancer. No one living there should neglect the opportunity; increasingly few do. The treatment, centred upon the Christie

Hospital, is universally acknowledged to be excellent. Under the leadership of Professor Noel Clark, a redoubtable team of consultants is extending the repertoire of treatments available to combat a condition that has become, for many men, a virtually inevitable introduction to old age.

So it was that, following my biopsy, I was scheduled to meet, not Professor Clark himself, but Dr. Tony Elliott of his team. The meeting was scheduled, with a kind of biblical appositeness, for my seventieth birthday; not perhaps quite how I had intended to spend it. There is something awesome about reaching the biblical threescore years and ten, if also a sense of reaching harbour after a long voyage: a point at which life owes you nothing, and not much more can be expected of you: a place of rest. I viewed the forthcoming consultation with resignation, not alarm.

But I received a preparatory call from the delightful Louise, the MacMillan nurse who coordinates my treatment. She informed me that prostate cancers are assessed for aggressiveness on a scale of 6-10 (why start at 6?) and that mine had been graded 10, the highest score. Many of my friends would say that this was only to be expected, given my character in general. It came, though, as something of a shock to find that, for the first time in my life, I had a tiger between my legs. Louise continued,

"Dr Elliott will want to discuss with you the possibility of offering you chemotherapy. Often, gentlemen have difficulty with this, but you must now realize that you are part of a high-risk group."

Better and better! Of course, I discussed this interesting revelation with my wife, who immediately, and predictably, adopted a pro-chemo stance. Anything that was (a) potentially life-prolonging and (b) free should be seized upon. I was not at first disposed to agree; I harboured memories of Margaret's own chemotherapy treatment, for breast cancer, twelve years earlier. At 70, I wasn't sure that the game remained worth the candle.

I went into my meeting with Dr.Elliott, then, in a state of some uncertainty; also some discomfort. The biopsy had stirred up my urinary tract infection, yet again. Long meetings were suddenly uncomfortable. I found Dr. Elliott approachable and impressive. He explained frankly that he found my cancer deeply puzzling. On that, at least, I shared his view.

"We really puzzled over this one. The scans show no sign of spread whatever, but in 25 years I have never seen a PSA score of 500 that didn't betoken SOME spread. I frankly don't believe the scans; I think there must be little bits of cancer too microscopic to detect, and I want to proceed on that basis."

At this point, Margaret interjected:

"Oh for God's sake, don't spoil the only bit of good news we've had!"

Dr Elliott had the good grace to look slightly shamefaced at this. He was not the only doctor to find my symptoms paradoxical; several seemed to find it slightly irritating to have their expectations so rudely confounded.

I however was impressed : to follow one's gut instinct and experience, rather than a number, seemed to me the essence of professionalism. I also liked the idea of playing safe. Dr.Elliott went on to explain what chemotherapy would entail – six sessions of exposure to a drug called docetaxel, recently introduced for the treatment of breast cancer, but beginning to be used for prostate cancer on an experimental basis. The drug is highly toxic, and the experience unpleasant, but early results are moderately encouraging. The hormone therapy would continue, and radiotherapy would follow the chemo.

Dr.Elliott did not attempt to "sell" this course of treatment; he merely presented the pros and cons dispassionately, in the context of what was clearly some uncertainty about the actual nature of my condition. I decided to go for the chemotherapy as much because I knew it was Margaret's heartfelt wish as because I was convinced it was necessary. At this stage I was much reassured by the lack of drama attending every consultation. For the NHS staff, it was very much business as usual. I did not do the usual thing, which is to ransack Google for information about my condition; nor did I ask for a prognosis (and I would not have welcomed one). So far as I was concerned, my future was now in more expert hands.

The treatment did not begin at once. There was time to celebrate my birthday, slightly belatedly, in Venice, again with David and Patsy. I think my favourite place in the world, increasingly so as I get older, is the island of Torcello in the Venice Lagoon. A thousand years ago, it was a rich and bustling place, and a great, almost intact, Byzantine cathedral stands as testimony to its grandeur. Now the place is almost entirely abandoned to birdlife and the sound of the wind rustling in the reeds. A few dozen people live there, and there are two or three small, rather refined, inns and a couple of discrete restaurants. It is a place for silence and reflection upon mortality, and the consolation that there is great beauty in decay. Once I was there, sipping a chocolate and a great crowd of people wandered past, no doubt from some cruise ship. I walked to the cathedral with a sinking heart, thinking I would find it crowded with gaudy tee-shirts and expensive odours. In fact, no one was to be seen. It was as though the gawking tourists had been absorbed into the silence and obscurity of the place.

There, in the rose garden of the Locanda Cipriani, on a sweetly warm May afternoon beside the cathedral, we celebrated my birthday, the four of us, with a simple lunch and a local white wine. I thought that, if this was to be my last birthday, it was the best place and best company I could have chosen.

There was also time to think about some of the aesthetic consequences of my treatment. I should at once say that I am no oil painting; closer to an oil slick, some would say. I am not, however, totally without vanity, and I did not look forward to losing my hair. I therefore made an appointment with a wigmaker, though of course he did not call himself anything so mundane: I think "practical trichological solutions" was the preferred description. He turned out to be an old chap, working from a garage in Westhoughton, who had built a worldwide business on covering up people's bald patches: he had, it transpired, a factory in Shanghai. I did not speculate on the reasons why human hair might be more readily forthcoming in the People's Republic of China than elsewhere. His way of doing business was to talk at length about himself and to interpose discouraging comments from time to time:

"Are you sure you want a wig? You probably won't look any worse bald."

But I persevered, finally handing over five hundred quid for a grey wig that has since sat on a bookshelf, treated with great suspicion by our cats, who think it may be a rival. Armed with this cosmetic prophylactic, I had my head shaved by a rather lovely hairdresser. I enjoyed the process rather more than the result, but the hairdresser, lying gallantly, said "you look great." So did others of my acquaintance. I shall never believe any of them again.

My chemotherapy began a few days after our return at the Christie hospital, whither I proceeded, newly shorn of hair. The Christie, of course, is one of Europe's great centres for cancer research, as it is also one of Manchester's great institutions. Forty years ago, I used to pass it every day on my way to Manchester Grammar School. There is rather more of it now than there was then, as is true also of MGS (and indeed of me). It is my greatest good fortune to live less than an hour's drive from the Christie.

I was immediately taken by the atmosphere of the place. The outpatient clinics are bright, modern and comfortable. By definition, rather a large proportion of the patient body is dying, but the ethos is neither gloomy, nor especially sepulchral. People come, not to die, but to prolong life, and to grasp at what life has left to offer. On an early visit, I drank coffee with an elderly couple who had been coming for eight years, as the wife's condition recurred. It was clear that they had come to regard it, not so much as a place of treatment, as a club. As is true of all hospitals, the staff are overworked, but not to the sickening extent that I observed in a Wolverhampton hospital where my sister was treated, and the nurses lacked the time even to observe the full range of safety measures. At the Christie, the staff seemed proud of their work, and proud to be there. One evening, as I was leaving rather late, I remarked to a cleaner that I had never been in so spotlessly clean a hospital. She positively swelled with pride in response.

Each bout of treatment began with a blood test, to check that one was actually in sufficient health to endure the rigours about to be inflicted. The decision to treat or not to treat was in the hands of a senior clinical practitioner, not a doctor. In my case, this was a good-looking, rather jolly chap of Asian origin called Cam. He took a robust view of treatment, wrapping nothing up. Chemotherapy is in effect a systematic course of poisoning undertaken in the hope that the cancer will succumb before the patient. Steroids must be taken before and after treatment to control after-effects, and one is required to inject oneself in the abdomen with further drugs for a week after treatment. A picnic it is not, but the physical circumstances are at least comfortable. The treatment room resembles a high-end hairdressing salon, with comfortably padded reclining chairs, which invariably in my case induced sleep. A drip is attached to one or other arm (of the patient, not the chair), and a nurse looks sagely at a dial from time to time. Then you go.

I cannot honestly say I had much to do with my fellow patients, who changed at every visit. I remember a man from somewhere in the Rossendale Valley, who had willed all his money to the Christie. He had allowed his prostate condition to worsen to the extent that he had been rushed unconscious to the hospital, which had certainly saved his life. I remember hearing another man engaged in an altercation with a nurse, because he refused to take his steroids or administer his abdominal injections, and could not therefore be treated. The injections certainly present some difficulty to many patients. My problem was excess of vigour. I had to be reminded that these were intended to be merely subcutaneous: it was unnecessary to skewer oneself.

The effects of docetaxel are not instantaneous. On each visit, I was able to walk to the car, with no more than a slight fuzziness in my head. The steroids kicked in first, giving rise to an extraordinary restlessness that made sleep quite impossible the first night after treatment. Happily, one such wakeful night coincided with the 2017 General Election, which I was able to follow with a mixture of patriotic dismay and glee at the discomfiture of the hapless Theresa May. The fourth day after treatment was always a trial: a dreadful lethargy set in, accompanied by a feeling that one's veins were boiling. This lasted, with diminishing force for about a week; the second week saw a gradual improvement; the third, a return to something close to normality. I was able to walk a mile or two and exercise gently in the gym, where I think my presence may have been something of an embarrassment to my fellow gymnasts, who competed to tell me how well I was looking. Much later, my friend Lance confessed,

"I was lying mate. You looked like shit."

I had rather suspected that, but it was good to have it in Lance's incomparable terminology.

In general, I was moved by the overwhelming kindness I received. This manifested itself in many offers of transport and, among my female friends, in a positive orgy of baking. I lived for some weeks on banana cake. A systematic effort was made to keep my spirits up, sometimes with some difficulty. One of Margaret's friends later confessed that each time she had seen me, she had wept on leaving, precisely because, as Lance would have it, I looked "like shit."

None of it was unbearable. On each visit to the Christie, my blood was in mint condition, and Cam commented on my generally robust condition:

"I can hardly believe you've had chemotherapy."

I was not depressed; I sank into no slough of self-pity. If I felt sorrow, it was engendered by the incompetence of the England cricket team, not by my physical condition.

Never give way to the temptation to believe that things can't get any worse. They always can. Now, they did.

Margaret had for some months been troubled by what she at first thought was a return of the haemorrhoids by which she has been occasionally troubled over the years. The usual remedies for piles, however, had no effect. The discomfort got worse, to the point where a visit to the GP could no longer be avoided. The GP was concerned:

"It's probably nothing, but I'm going to refer you to the hospital under the 14 day rule."

So once again the spectre of cancer was raised. Margaret duly went to be examined by a specialist, who I suppose was a proctologist (a term it has long been my ambition to use in a serious context). I have been very fortunate in the medical staff I have seen: all have been friendly, open and approachable. The practice of proctology is perhaps not conducive to a particularly jolly approach to life, but the gentleman in question radiated a kind of sepulchral competence. As we were waiting, his secretary whispered to us, "Mr X doesn't wrap things up." Following an examination, he announced that a biopsy would be needed, but that he was almost certain that there was "a little skin cancer" (the diminutive suggested a certain affection) "in there somewhere."

Margaret then proceeded, as is her wont on these occasions, to ask all the questions to which you don't want an answer:

"What kind of cancer?"

"I can't say."

"What's the worst it could be?"

"It could be an ano-rectal melanoma."

This of course, had it been true, was the worst possible news. Melanomas are frisky little cancers, almost invariably fatal. Margaret interpreted this as a death sentence. I pointed out in vain that the specialist had NOT made any such diagnosis, though he might have gone further in pointing out how very rare such cancers are. At any rate, a grisly few weeks ensued, as we waited for the results of a biopsy which showed that the cancer was a squameous carcinoma: extremely nasty, but curable.

At this point, I admit that we had begun to believe that things couldn't get much worse. Which of course they did. One Thursday morning our cat Bertie came to meet our cleaner. He always did, with the attention of assisting in her work which would, without his cooperation, have been completed in half the time. Clearly he was, as always, looking forward to a morning of uninhibited mayhem. Ten minutes later, Margaret found him at the foot of a bed, quite dead. Marie, the cleaner, attempted to give him mouth to mouth resuscitation; not a thing I would have attempted. Dearly as I loved Bertie, his habit of licking his nether regions would have deterred me from any such intimate contact.

We both agree that this was the worst moment of all those we experienced in a grim year. Bertie was about as idiotic as a cat can be, but he was also overwhelmingly affectionate, gentle and mischievous. We paid to have him autopsied; this was a mistake: to read a report which referred to him throughout as "the carcasse" was heart-rending. This was, after all, the lovely creature that came to lie on my chest each night, gazing lovingly into my eyes. He was a delight, and I miss him even now, eighteen months later. Marie commented on the morning of his death that she had never seen a man so distressed.

Whether there is any connection or not, I cannot say, but it was about this time that the effects of the docetaxel really began to be felt. My fourth treatment left me for a few days unable to walk more than a few paces without becoming exhausted. I remember our calling at a garden centre for lunch, and wondering if I could make the short journey from the car park. The lethargy was such that each step was almost too great an effort to make. If someone had told me that I was at that point twenty minutes from death, I would have believed them, and the news would have been welcome. A number of unwelcome symptoms made their appearance: the tingling in my fingers that I had felt from my first treatment gave way to a numbness that felt permanent, as has proved to be the case; I felt occasional nausea; worst of all my balance was affected, to the point where I could not remain on the spot without feeling strongly inclined to topple over.

Neither Margaret nor I is a natural nurse. Both of us, I think, would have preferred the role of patient to that of carer. As it was, we were both dangerously ill, and neither of us was in a position to look after the other. Severe as my treatment was, moreover, it swiftly became apparent that Margaret's would be worse. It was described for us at the Christie by the formidable Dr.Alam – an attractive young woman of great intelligence, who appears to have cornered the market in anal cancers. It appeared that the position of the cancer was such as to make surgery inadvisable: the risk of causing incontinence was just too great. Since the cancer could not be cut out, it would need to be burnt out by a combination of chemotherapy and radiotherapy administered concurrently over a short period culminating in ten days of therapy which, we were assured, would be painful ("think of the worst sunburn you've ever had and multiply it by ten"), but would be likely to lead to cure. Cure! Not a word readily associated with cancer treatment, which attempts rather to keep you alive for long enough to allow you to die of something else.

It was now early summer. Margaret asked if she would be able to go on the trip to Athens we had planned for September.

"No chance. For the next six months you belong to us. You certainly won't feel like sitting on a plane. In fact, you won't feel like sitting at all."

At least we knew. As we left, I overheard a couple arranging their transport back from the hospital (which provides transport for patients who have none), and wearily realising that their journey home, though not very far, would take four hours. By contrast, we drove to Didsbury for a pleasant meal then headed home, forty minutes away. Having cancer is no joke, but being poor and having cancer is a lot worse.

We were left with the quandary of who would look after whom. Even this is to ignore our most demanding domestic duty, which is to satisfy the demands of our surviving cat, Buster. Margaret's old friend, Patsy, volunteered to come and stay. This was not only generous but extremely enticing, since Patsy cooks to professional standards. However, no sooner had she made the offer than she went down with a chest infection that made it impossible for her to come near us for several months.

Margaret then decided that she would accept the offer of a bed in the Christie for the key part of her treatment. Simultaneously, another Patsy stepped into the breach made by the illness of the first Patsy. My dear friends David and Patsy Hinchliffe offered to take me into their home just outside Taunton for the duration of Margaret's stay in hospital, while Val, another old friend, accepted the rather more demanding responsibility for Buster. I shall never forget this generosity, and can never adequately repay it.

And, for the only time in my life, I was in need of care. I turned up for my fifth bout of chemotherapy for Cam to greet me:

"God, you look terrible. I can't believe it's the same man."

I described for him what had been a miserable three weeks, and it was immediately decided that I would not go on to the planned sixth and final session. There is a bell for you to ring as you leave the chemo unit for the last time. I did so with a mixture of relief and apprehension. While there, I felt I was in trusted hands. Now I was on my own.

Off I went then to the West Country, while Margaret took up residence in the Christie. She dismissed my concern at my inability to visit:

"I'll have loads of visitors every day. I'd much rather see Marion or Therese, and you're a bloody useless hospital visitor anyway. You just stand around looking miserable. I'd rather just not have to worry about you."

And so, I had a delightful week with my friends, while she endured tortures which she has subsequently been unwilling to describe in any depth. When David and I went to collect her, she looked more fragile than I would have thought possible, after so short a period of treatment. The initial signs were, however, that the treatment had worked.

It was time to look forward to radiotherapy. Throughout the six months or so that had elapsed since my biopsy, I had taken an antibiotic as a prophylactic against the return of a urinary tract infection. Reasoning that the UTI would not survive the therapy, I fatuously decided to omit the antibiotic for the duration. This turned out to be an uncomfortable and nearly fatal mistake.

In introducing the radiotherapy – compering the show, so to speak – Dr Elliott warned me that there would be some side-effects:

"You may find yourself urinating a bit more often. Usually the effects fade quite quickly once the treatment is over, but there may be some after-effects for life."

He added that it wasn't possible to direct the beam with absolute accuracy, so that some effects on the bowel might also be possible. This, clearly, was going to be fun.

My radiotherapy lasted through November 2017. It was, as is customary in the north-west, a damp autumn, the streets soft with the mulch of fallen leaves which the council is too strapped for cash to have swept, the rain falling insistently, not hard, but insinuating. Salford Council in this case. My therapy was administered at the Christie Unit in Salford Royal Hospital. I had never been to the hospital before. More than most such establishments, it is schizophrenic in style: a gleaming modern building attached to an original Victorian pile, with no effort at coherence.

The RT unit is agreeably separate from the main buildings. It has its own barrier and its own carpark. For the modest (and returnable) sum of five pounds, they will give you a key-fob that lets you raise the barrier. The carpark is then free, and almost always has spaces. That was a considerable relief: going to a hospital is inevitably a somewhat alarming experience; having to compete with other drivers for the last remaining square foot of space makes it more so.

Once more, I had the sense of being especially well looked-after – of having become a VIP through the very accident (which I found effortless) of getting cancer. The waiting room at the unit is like the lobby of a four-star hotel; one feels like a valued customer, not a damn nuisance for whom a plastic chair might grudgingly be made available, if forced. There is a pleasant café, selling robustly unhealthy food, and a receptionist who greets you with a friendly smile, rather than the traditional suspicious leer.

The treatment is initially somewhat alarming. You receive an introductory talk which lays great stress on the condition of your bowels. This is not with me a favourite topic of conversation, but I tried not to resent having this peculiarly embarrassing form of introspection forced upon me. I then emerged from the talk clutching, slightly mystified, a box of Movicol sachets. It appeared that the prostate changes position slightly depending on whether the bowels are empty of full. In order to facilitate aiming of the beam, bowel consistency is required. What a lot I was learning about the more dubious functions of the human body! The bladder similarly was required to be as empty as humanly possible.

The patient (in this case me) was required to remove trousers and enter a large room where various figures in green surrounded a machine that might have been, but wasn't, a giant trouser press. The greeting was always the same:

"Name?

Date of birth?

First line of address?"

This I took to be a precaution against any intruder who might be there for the purpose of securing treatment to which he was not entitled. Following this ritual, one lay on a hard couch, whereupon two attendants manoeuvred one's limbs into a position of maximum discomfort and instructed one on no account to move. Following this, the green-suited ones fled behind a screen, and the machine hummed into action. A semi-circular bit hovered in predatory fashion over one's tackle, moving slowly first clockwise then anticlockwise. There was no sensation, other than a modest ache in one's shoulder-blades from the couch. After a short time, relief came:

"That's it for now. Have a nice day. See you tomorrow."

This happened twenty times, without variation, other than a couple of meetings with a head nurse who enquired as to any after-effects, and then ignored the answers.

The impact on me was immediate, and much more rigorous than I had been led to expect. I suspect that my decision to stop the antiobiotic may have been at fault. The UTI came back, so that a sump of diseased liquid in my bladder was in effect being microwaved on a daily basis. Within a few days, I was peeing every fifteen minutes. After a couple of weeks, I was in such excruciating discomfort that I could only sleep hunched in a chair, covered in a blanket. This was good news for Buster, who repeatedly bit my toes as they protruded from the blanket.

No help was forthcoming. I think now that this was entirely my fault, as I failed entirely to communicate to the staff how much trouble I was in fact in. I accepted facile reassurance:

"It's all quite normal"

Or inadequate palliatives:

"Drink cranberry juice."

"Take Paracetamol."

Margaret, of course, bore the brunt of my self-pity, at the very time when she was in some consistent discomfort herself.

The treatment ended, but the effects lingered on, and in fact got worse. As a reward for their generosity, we treated David and Patsy to a short holiday in Prague, when I was still in such excruciating pain that I can only have been the most dismal company. I am not, admittedly, normally the life and soul of the party, but when I am feeling sorry for myself I yield to noone in my capacity to communicate misery.

This dire position continued over Christmas and into the New Year, Finally, thinking that surely RT could not ordinarily be this bad, I contacted my GP, who sensibly said,

"The first thing to do is to find out if there is an infection there."

Obediently, I went off to the surgery to demand one of their sample kits; I flatter myself that I have no equal in the operation of these squalid but necessary implements. Thus enclosed, my urine winged its way through the ether to the pathology laboratory at the Royal Bolton Hospital.

Before the results were received, events became somewhat more melodramatic than I altogether like to recall. I woke at 2am one morning, still sitting on the couch, trembling uncontrollably and freezing cold. I telephoned Margaret, who was asleep in her room above. She tells me that she found me barely coherent and, finding this unusual, decided to phone an ambulance. I vaguely remember the journey to hospital, but vividly recall what happened there. I was at once diagnosed with sepsis, filled with antibiotics and sentenced to be catheterised. The sentence was carried out by a young female doctor, who had clearly learned her trade on the hockey pitches of some distinguished school. The insertion was difficult and took at least five attempts. The doctor's approach to difficulties can perhaps best be summed up in the phrase "give it some welly". It was the most excruciating few minutes I have known.

I was lucky. Worldwide, one in three people who get sepsis die of it. I spent only one night in hospital and had the catheter in me for just a month; my kidney function was initially damaged but quickly recovered. The catheter was a nuisance and offered possibilities of humiliation which were not, in the end, fully realised. There have been some misadventures subsequently, but the history of a man's urinary function quickly loses its entertainment value. It is best to pass over the next few months.

# PRESENT AND FUTURE

At the moment, life is not too bad. I participate in one of the many research projects on the subject of prostate cancer. As part of my contribution, I am required to complete a questionnaire on my health every three months. When asked to score my quality of life on a scale of 1-10, I currently rate it 7 or 8. Ten months ago, it was 3-4.

So, things are better than they were. I still experience a number of side-effects of my treatment. The hormone treatment causes hot flushes, tiredness and, occasionally, depression which manifests itself in an emotionalism that was never entirely foreign to my nature, but is now much more extreme. For the first time in my life, I weep easily. I am not as strong or well-coordinated as I was. There are still after effects of the chemo- and radiotherapy: my finger tips are numb, my nails tend to grow too thick and to dig into the flesh of my fingers; worse, I still need to use the lavatory far too frequently, including several visits each night. For much of the time, I feel a low level of discomfort in bladder and bowel.

All these symptoms are, however, minor. I can live a normal life, go where I want, exercise as I wish, travel abroad. I can go to the cinema, though I remain reluctant to risk the theatre or a concert, for fear that I would need to leave and that my exit would cause disruption. I have never been especially prone to enjoyment, but I find myself appreciating the mysterious accident of consciousness more than I used to. Simple things make a significant impression: the feel of sunshine, the wind on my face, the sensation of movement, the warmth of a hot shower on my skin. Sometimes I pick up my cat and press him to my cheek, feeling his small body throb with what I hope is pleasure, though it may equally be resentment. Cats are like that. I gain positive enjoyment from sensations I previously hardly noticed: putting on warm clothes, eating a tea-cake, watching a dog hurtle round a lawn with the sheer joy of being alive.

My life has been a fortunate one. I often regret that I have not had children, though when I observe the difficulties several of my friends have experienced with their children and grandchildren, I am not so sure. I have been loved, I have good friends whom I love in return; I have worked with stimulating colleagues on important things; I have enough money to do most of what I would like to do. I might have done more, achieved more; that I have not is, I accept, my own fault. I am now 71, and do not feel that life owes me anything.

The future is uncertain: at 71, it is bound to be somewhat restricted in extent. Cancer will restrict it further, though I do not know how much, nor do I want to know. However, I have already lived 36 years longer than Mozart and 43 more than Masaccio.

Death is the debt we all owe for this miraculous experience of having been conscious in a world packed with beauty. I do not think I fear it, though I worry that the process of arriving at it may be somewhat messy. Intellectually, I accept the arguments first expressed, so far as I know by Epicurus and restated by Lucretius: that it is irrational to fear death because, following the cessation of life, there is nothing left to experience pain (or anything else). I reflect also that the universe is, according to the latest calculations, some 13.8 billion years old. For 13, 799, 999, 929 of those years, I was not alive; that is, dead. I do not recall, in all that vast abyss of time, ever having been in the slightest perturbed by the trivial matter of my non-existence.

Matter is indestructible, but subject to transformation governed by such rules as the second law of thermodynamics. All that I am composed of originated as star-dust, and it will be recycled. I therefore look forward to joining Johann Sebastian Bach in that tree. I wonder what I shall talk to him about.

At least, I think this is what I feel. I am in no danger of succumbing to a deathbed conversion. To surrender to what I believe to be a delusion would be pusillanimous indeed. Nor do I think anyone is likely to inflict Extreme Unction upon me, as happened to Evelyn Waugh's Lord Marchmain. And yet, I am not quite perfectly stoical.

In the Nordic television series "The Bridge," an obnoxious young journalist finds himself trapped in a car by an ingenious and sadistic terrorist. The car is, to all appearances, booby-trapped. In a few minutes, it will explode. A loudly ticking clock warns the journalist that his life expectancy has become suddenly and brutally abbreviated. The police duly arrive to rescue him and extract from him vital information. Their efforts are unavailing. At last, with two minutes to go, they retire to a safe distance. At that point, the lead detective, a young woman who has Asperger's syndrome (an indispensable qualification for a detective in a Scandinavian drama), rings the journalist and tries to persuade him to divulge his information. He may as well, she explains, for there is nothing to fear; the action of the explosive will be far too rapid for him to feel pain: his constituent molecules will be dispersed across much of Sweden long before his nervous system has time to react. This does nothing to reassure the journalist, who continues to scream and beat uselessly on the windows of the car. In the end, it proves to be a hoax; the clock stops ticking, the doors of the car open, and the journalist totters out. He is not so lucky in a later episode.

I ask myself whether I would behave with perfect calm in such circumstances, and I fear the answer is that I would not. The detective's argument is impeccable, but I do not know whether I would be quite convinced that being blown apart would be a completely painless experience. There is also a certain awfulness about the prospect of non-existence. Christopher Hitchens, reflecting on his own death, which he knew to be imminent, quotes with (somewhat qualified) approval, Philip Larkin's "Aubade."

The sure extinction that we travel to

And shall be lost in always. Not to be here,

Not to be anywhere,

And soon; nothing more terrible, nothing more true..

And specious stuff that says *no rational being*

*Can fear a thing it will not feel,* not seeing

That this is what we fear.

This expresses, I think, perhaps in rhetoric that is slightly too pat and in antitheses that are slightly too sharply drawn, a fear as universal as fear of the dark.

Yet there are fears to which it is the responsibility of the rational being not to give way. It is, I think, simply untrue that there is nothing more terrible than non-existence; excess of life is more terrible. The prolongation of life beyond the point at which it is possible to live usefully and with dignity is a far worse prospect than that of death.

In our time, the prolongation of life has become surrounded by a kind of semi-religious fervour. Just as the ancient Egyptians embalmed their dead for eternity in a quest for the after-life, so we embark upon an even more self-evidently futile quest for immortality in this life. We exercise religiously, we eat a diet more suited to a fruit-bat than a human being, we pay huge sums of money to the purveyors of various kinds of snake-oil, we enfeeble ourselves by our anxiety to avoid stress, we worry ourselves into insomnia through concern that we cannot sleep, we feel shame at our weaknesses, even at the inevitable depredations of age. We direct towards the obese, the drunk, the couch potato the hatred previous societies directed at the heretic. We shun death, we cover it in body bags, we teach our children to look away. Death is not merely "the blight man was born for;" it is a social solecism of the most heinous kind. Even funerals have become "celebrations of life," because we cannot accept that the star performer is in fact dead.

It is better to feel that:

> Man must abide his going hence,

> Even as his coming hither. Ripeness is all.

I do not feel fear, or resentment, or sorrow at the thought that I shall be dead before too long.

There is an old lady called Hilda who lives near us. She is over eighty, and not well, but she is not given to complaint. Once, she was greeted in a shop with these words,

> Eee, Hilda, you always seem so cheerful.

"Aye," she replied, "you 'ave ter be. If you ain't no bugger's gonna do owt about it, are they?"

Just so. She has not the language, like Larkin to bleat about how terrible it all is. In the last few years, she has had little enough reason to be happy. Her husband was an active man well into old age. He loved to walk on the high moors that surround our town, striding for miles with sheep, clouds, and the odd alarmed skylark for company. He would watch the buzzards wheeling above with their oddly pathetic kitten's cry, and he would look down over Greater Manchester to the Peak District, or further off to the mountains of Snowdonia. But Alzheimer's took away his nimbleness and all his capacity for quiet joy, and when he died, it was a mercy, but not an unequivocal one. Hilda grieved for him, not with bitterness, rather with gratitude for a long and loving marriage and a kind companion.

"Eee, I did cry," she said to Margaret when he died. All the sadness of late widowhood, all the sorrow of happiness past is in these quiet, self-deprecating words. There will be no recovery from this loss, nor should there be.

But it speaks of a cowardice of which Hilda is not guilty to call this "terrible." It is simply the way of the world. I shall die, because I was born. I did not ask to be born, but I am glad that I was, and Hilda has given me her husband's rucksack and maps as a reminder of the need for stoicism.

I have two caveats. I feel sorrow not for me, but for those I leave behind: a dear woman in an empty house, beloved friends with a gap in their Christmas card list and, perhaps, in their thoughts. And I should like my little cat, Buster, to be buried with me. His presence in Elysium, if it exists, would comfort me, and he might, in a better world, give as much thought to pleasing me as he does to pleasing himself. No, I don't believe it either.

## Chemotherapy

This is what, at twenty, I thought
That seventy would be; it is,
Thank heaven, mostly not: slow,
Sapping, sluggish not-quite- pain
Impeding the limbs, cluttering the brain;
Every incline become a hill, each hill
An ornament to be observed, beyond
Ambition; words more flirtatious
Than they were, fluttering out of reach,
Not quite recalled: appetites mostly gone,
Sleep fugitive and brief; long days
On sofas pillowing in books.

And yet, some things remain:
A pianissimo high A, perfect
In a tenor's throat, released,
Like a vaulting bird a hundred
Years ago, immortal in fragility;
Or the play of light on a distant field
Of wind-combed corn; the lifting
Of cloud off Lakeland Fells across the sea:
The look, sometimes, of admiration
In a beloved eye that seems to say,
You have much to tolerate, old friend.
I think you bear it well.

## Awake

Midnight is sounding:
An owl flies across the moon,
But sleep does not come.

Naked and alone,
I am distant from the dawn,
Yet it is all I have.

Breeze caresses me
Gently from the kindly night,
But sleep does not come.

## Relief

My friend Wally
Went to hospital in June.
He hadn't peed since January,
Or shat since Halloween.
They sat him down, they did,
Down on a commode,
And filled him up with this and that,
And waited till he shat.

And now he is a lighter man;
He passed a brick or two,
Emptying his hairy bum,
Like a rhino at a zoo.

## Seventy

Three-score years and ten;
Soixante-neuf will not come again.
No reason to complain.
What's left is the dark plain
That follows the downward slide,
The shift from side to side
Of tiny irritations, minor aches
That may foreshadow the sudden break
Of little vessels in the brain,
The darkness come again
That lasted since the universe began,
Lifted a moment and shuttered down:
All you were and are and would ever be
In the blessed amnesia of eternity.

## Being well

People keep telling me how well I look.
They may be surprised to find me
Still alive. I thank them, politely as I can
And agree that, yes, I thrive. I shall not
Always do so. I hear small sharp claws
Above me in the attic, scratching to get in,
To where I lie awake. The wind
Finds wormholes in my cottage wall,
Where small birds lived and bred
That now are gone into the dark mystery
Of the winter night. I am not afraid,
But curious in the vicinity
Of death. And I look well. It must be so.
I have the testimony of those who,
Loving me, wish that it were so.

## Walking Again

I am learning to walk again.
The last time, I could fall,
And nobody minded;
No one at all.

I am learning to walk again.
No one taught me before;
Now everyone does,
Not like before.

I am learning to walk again,
And am not permitted to fall;
And mustn't hurt myself.
No dear, not at all.

But the planet has shifted away.
The earth isn't there any more.
And gravity is twice
What it ever was before.

## At the Christie

The Christie yesterday:
Bright, cheerful, no hint of despair;
I like going there,
Though you carry pain away;
They do not let you leave it there,
And as you leave, smiling ladies,
Black and plump and sweet-scented,
Wipe the walls clean of worried breath,
And the stale exhalations
Of waiting for deaths that may
Come soon, but not perhaps today.
Death is normal, accept that it is so,
And smile, it seems to say.

## Not the same

I have become an imposter
Impersonating me.
"You don't seem to be
The same man," they say:
People I meet, and have not met
This last long week or two.
"Who do I seem to you,"
I want to say, "And do you pity
Me, or someone else, here
Yet other than I am. No,
I am not what I was,
But then, I never was,
And nor were you. Merely,
I go on, obdurately.
There is nothing else to do.'

## Peripheral neuropathy

I think my fingers will fall off soon.
Not all of them, just the bits
I used to feel with, frostbitten
In the last surprising ebb of summer.
Perhaps I should cut them away, paring
Away the dead flesh, as explorers do,
Marching to a pole; it hardly matters which
Ocean or continent, the black stumps lie
Imperishable in ice. Dissolution is
More painful than I expected it to be
And quicker. The blackness climbs
From joint to joint, a blight upon me,
A Dutch-elm disease all my very own;
I must sit and enjoy it, while I can.

## Autumn 2017

Bead-bright, autumn brings clarity,
Cleansed skies, Perseid clustered,
Crowded with constellations. Cold
Pinches faces raisin-dry, old
And anxious. England disappears
Under rotting vegetation, words
Uttered by imbeciles, abandoned hopes,
The betrayed futures of the young,
The useless accumulation of the old.
Public men mouth apologies
For offences they did not intend
And do not regret. The shrill voices
Of the professionally indignant
Demand a recourse they do not
Deserve, and cannot define. England,
In this gaudy rottenness , is lost,
Its bland surface suddenly bright
With a seedy glamour. Autumn
Is here, and April will not come.

## Waking in hospital

I woke to a kaleidoscope of smells:
The exhalations of dying men,
Broken wind, broken sweat, a sweetness
Somewhere, half-hinted, of yesterday.
Disguised in some cheap unguents,
A harshness of carbolic or disinfectant,
All eddying around my own stink
Of having brushed too close to death.

I woke to sussurations, sliding sounds
Of men in slippers, not quite fitting,
Shuffling over polished floors
To impossibly distant lavatories
And to sighs escaping from those
Still sleeping parallel, in stupor
Opioid induced and heavy
With elusive oblivion.

I woke to a strange light, pearly
And oddly comforting, gathered
Not shed, like a mist or cloud
Assembled from a hill. And I lay,
Feeling a joy of absolute surrender
To what the dawning day might bring;
And each day since, on wakening,
I have sought that light again, in vain.

## Energy

There is nothing I want to do today.
The world has spread its treasures
Before me. I have motioned them away.
There is nothing I want to do today.
Doing nothing is one of the many things
I don't want to do today. It is too hard
To live in the infinitesimal slowness
Of an ageing world and not look for something.
And if not nothing, there must be something
One might do. A purpose, a meaning in life.
But life is not a proposition, and can have
No meaning. Purposes used to appeal to me
When I was steely, young and bright
And faintly Prussian. Now I see
That life goes on indifferent to any conceit
With which I garland it. We make
No difference. I think perhaps
That I shall sleep today: not nothing,
But nothing very much.

## Chemotherapy Lies

You're looking better today,
Better now your hair's come back.
Smiling encouragement, that's what they say;
But it's exactly what they said before,
When I was balder than a billiard ball.
Embarrassed by my nakedness,
Cancer made liars of them all.
And though I look healthier now,
More hirsute, a "better colour",
Still, I am slowly dying
And shall not cease doing so,
For all their well-meant lying.

## A flummoxed Onc

He told me that my PSA was high:
Himalaya-high, a score
Hardly ever seen before,
Yet, even to the practised eye,
The scans revealed no spread.
Bemused, the oncologist said,
There really should be spread:
If there were no spread, he said,
It would counter every rule,
Break every precedent,
And make an utter fool
Of the indisputably eminent.
It must be there, it has to be
Lurking somewhere within,
To think otherwise, believe you me,
Would be worse than sin.

## Lazarus

"You're looking great, " they say,
"Fantastic. I remember why
I fancied you, forty years ago."
Embarrassed, I mutter something
English and non-committal. "You
Must have lost a lot of weight."
"It must be somewhere," I confirm,
"I shall, no doubt, find it again
Before too long." They go on,
"You must be so relieved." "Yes,
Frequently," I reply, recalling nights
Inseparable from the porcelain
Confronting my materiality
With a reluctant stream. Back
To life, like a miner disinterred,
Focus of a thousand gazes,
Wondering how it feels:
The hot and stinking breath
Of mortality. "Oh, you do look
Well, " they say, meaning only,
"You are not dead, I see."
And I? I know what they do not,
And hide my deadly knowledge
In my failing heart.

## I cried

"I cried when I saw you last,"
She said, "struggling to rise:
The look of death was in your cheeks
And night was in your eyes."

I never knew she cared for me
Or that she felt such grief.
She seemed indifferent,
Or that was my belief.

"I did not know I touched you so,"
I said," struggling to rise.
Now I know what friends I had,
Much to my surprise."

## A Fall on a Fell

I did not see the stone that suddenly
Thrust itself ahead of me.
It came from nowhere;
I was enjoying the cool air
And savouring the scenery
When it interrupted me
And pitched me, not seeing it,
Proverbial arse over tit.
I broke nothing at all,
But nothing broke my fall;
A very little blood was shed;
A few cells were scrambled in my head.
Now I know all too well
Why they call the bloody thing a fell.

OTHER POEMS

# Venice

Venice it must be, across the sea,
The quiet sea, the not-quite-sea,
The seeping in between low banks
Of water a man might wade in
If only he knew how and where.

Grey sky, grey water, scoured by trails
Of scurrying boats, quick and crushing
The tame and tentative ways, or slow
And nosing a path by black markers
Crowned by sharp-beaked gulls.

Even here, sea has its strange discipline,
Imposing an undue silence,
A slower rhythm, an impermanence
Of tidal flow and movement
Of adventitious migrant birds.

You cannot see the city yet
Past the grey sea and sodden islands
Where the bittern lurks
For those who know in salt marshes
And sharp-bladed reeds.

It is, though, rumoured to be there,
Recently reborn and bearing
The necklace of high tide
In celebration of its
Annual impossible resurrection.

Before you pass the walls of San Michele,
You see, rising from the sea,
Domes and towers of brick and stone,
Leaning in sympathy with the slow
Subsidence of piles and mud.

There is no glamour to be seen
From here, no rolling domes, no
Pink-marbled loggias, no horses
Preserved in brazen assertion
Of the sanctity of ancient theft.

As you come closer, instead, you see
Only the sobriety of high walls:
The Arsenale, the Ospedale
The Fondamente Nuove
With its cheap, expensive, restaurants.

The streets are narrow and crowded
With spectres of the living
And beside them the substantial dead,
Hurrying down the dark tunnels
Into the occasional sudden squares.

Because even here, life renews itself,
Children play in precious space,
Chasing, yelling, colliding, crashing
To the ground, competing for
Coloured balls with joyful, yapping dogs.

They do not know, these children
In their bright football shirts,
That they too are dying generations:
Piping thin, insubstantial ghosts
Flitting like images in memory.

The city trades on memory
And the gaudy images of decline:
Filigree Gothic is never far away:
Sudden yellow walls reflecting light
Off dappled gilt canals.

And yet, the genius of the place
Is loneliness: narrow streets,
Deserted squares, chill winds
Insinuating, blowing leaves
Off undiscovered trees.

We lived a week there
In that ambiguous loveliness
And renewed ourselves
In a kind of pious dedication
Ancient and ancestral,

Like city-dwellers venturing
Beyond the dark gates, to sit
By wayside sepulchres
On straight and sombre roads
To who knows where.

## The Dead Tit

Broken, its head large and limp,
Black on yellow, loose: flight
Forestalled by glass unseen.
Was it the bird I had seen,
Yesterday, in impromptu
Arabesques, pursuing
Gnats in the evening light?
Now, it merely rested unwarmed
In my hands, lifeless
As a message unreceived.

## McNair

Tommy McNair might as well
Not have been there;
Wasn't there, for all we knew,
We who do not see
The monsters of anonymity.
No one cared for him,
No one shared his privacy,
No one thought of him
No one knew the sharp edges
Of his boundless hate:
From the grey ocean
Of his anonymity, he fired
One assertion, centred
In loathing. How many more
Sit in neat houses, incubating
Atrocity in a womb of loneliness?

# The Grenfell Tower

Something not intended for heat
Burst, unpremeditated, into flame;
Fire, the God of Mischief, assumed
A temporary consuming reign.

He lit the expensive London sky
With an unaccustomed glory: red,
And yellow and cyanide blue;
And so the tower flamed high.

Flamed high in the costly London sky,
Beside the penthouses, the terraces
Of Regency white, the malls, the mews,
The ivied discretion; the rich.

The poor that had to die, died, consumed
In a Roman candle, placed for ornament,
But not for conflagration,
A monument to municipal greed.

A girl: wealthy, beautiful, tender-hearted,
Screamed her anger and despair,
For no more reason than humanity,
For those who perished there.

Men in Armani suits and Hermes ties
Piled food, blankets, toys in
Unconsidered heaps. In shows
Of undirected kindness, mindless charity.

"We care. We too can feel." They seemed to say,
In their undirected way:
For authority was otherwise occupied,
Thumb deep embedded in municipal arse.

Kindness undirected is wasted love,
Soaking useless in infertile ground.
We could do no more than stand around
And weep: for grief or anger? We hardly knew.

The hardly considered living became
Unconsidered dead, uncounted
Or uncontested, to spare the blushes
Of men grown evil through incompetence.

In the end, we may have them all:
The insect bodies, but not the names; some
Who died were there in hiding, others
Passing through, no rights at all.

No right to be on council property,
No right to that consuming blanket,
No right to sepulchre walls,
No right to recognition; none at all.

There is no democracy in death;
Some are mourned by millions,
Flattered in obituaries,
Oiled in elegies.

Others are blackened stumps,
Lying on blackened floors.
It will be an age before we remember them.
If we ever do.

## June Ending

June thickens into July;
Greens and yellows coalesce
And far-off mountains disappear.
In days now, if there is sun,
The rosebuds will release
In silent explosions
Their secret: that life goes on,
But will not tell us why.

## Not long

Not long to go now. Not long to go.
A Time, as in some drivelling aria,
To say goodbye. The Valkyries
Are massing somewhere in the sky;
Iris has her loft ladder ready to unroll,
Her lips wait to pluck the last breath,
As the swallow gleans the evening gnat.
Surely there should be more drama
In this ebbing of what began in fire
And in the dying of a star? No need
In this for protest, nothing to resent
Or fear. Acceptance? Yes and in
The mild onset of soon cessation,
A random wry thought: this too may disappoint.

## Bertie

Bertie died today. It was not his day
To die. We wondered why
He chose the day he did and why
So quietly. We found him on the floor
Looking quite content; caught us out,
Put one over on us yet once more.
Seven years we nurtured him;
Seven years we watched him grow
In size and strength, if not in sense.
He had the attributes of a cat:
Stubbornness, mischief, an incapacity
To learn. If he felt so inclined, he shat
Upon the kitchen floor, fell from open windows,
Destroyed computers, scratched lacquer
From the bedroom doors.
And for these virtues, and the honesty
In his great round amber eyes, the softness
Of his fur, his lulling gentle purr,
We loved him every moment he was alive.

# The Imagined Widow

Dorothy was in again.
I have given her that name;
She needed one. It suits
Her fur-edged coat and ankle boots.
As ever, she sits alone,
Wondering if she can afford a scone,
Sipping at her Earl Grey tea
In an alcove opposite me.

She covers her loneliness with a smile
And sits and thinks a while,
With her handbag on her knee,
Precious as memory,
Protected carefully
As quietly she sips her tea:
Bright and elderly and alone,
With grief as heavy as a stone.

She decides to have a scone,
Butters it as she sits alone,
Brushing the crumbs away
As she contemplates her day,
Her ring the only witness to her grief,
The indentation on her life
As on her finger; sitting alone,
Beside her tea and scone.

## Iris

She stands a while and looks,
Not through the glass,
But at the light, spreading
Through the ice on the inside
Of the pane, falling
Apart, as things do as they die,
A sudden rainbow
In the glancing sun.
And so, she looks for Iris
Gliding in splendour down,
And catches hopefully
A breath in her slender throat.

## Intense triviality

Maybe they are right, after all;
Maybe they always were:
The old man drawing lines
In grey symmetric pebbles,
Round and round a rock
That might have always been
There; a girl in a kimono setting
Flowers in a vase: one, then two,
Then three, no more, placing
And replacing, before arriving
At imagined perfection,
Unobserved; a woman
Folding a fastidious sheet
Tightly to a bed, the man
In a grey suit, pouring tea
As though dispensing eternity,
Deriving ceremony
From the trivial, meaning
From the banal: all these
Smiling contented, living
Where they are, in a moment
I have never sought to colonise.

## A reason to go

"A double room, with sea view,
Half-board, and a glass
Of prosecco." A thin stream
Of sickly effervescence
To charm the traveller,
Or woo the pilgrim: not
The fragment of the True Cross,
Not the Holy Grail, not the lance
That pierced a Saviour's side,
Only the vinegar, sweetened
To taste, to mock thirst
And dull unused senses.

## Listening

I was listening to Bach one day.
As the raindrops stormed the panes,
Pizzicato, the wind howled an obscene
Continuo. "Erbarme dich:" the clear line,
The virginal contralto, innocent
Of vibrato, spelled a mystery
I could not penetrate. Faith
Is not earned, but given, though
Not to me. And this is in itself
A mystery. And yet the subtle line,
Thin as smoke and rigorous
As a theorem, overcame
The storm and settled, wormlike,
In my brain, perhaps my soul,
In which I do not believe. The voice,
The violin, debated in language
As lovely as beyond comprehension,
Meaning nothing more to me
Than the random patter of the rain.

## Killing a mustelid

I was driving (North, I think).
I knew where I was going then,
That day, or thought I did.
I killed a weasel. I did not mean to;
Hardly saw him, swiftly as he slithered
Faster than a current down a wire.
I felt the small shock as my car
Passed over him. No one else did,
And he perhaps felt not as much.
One second and he lived, malignant
And assured; another, and he did not.
I remember him, limp and ragged
Indecipherable on the shining road.

## A Good Mother

A woman sat behind me in M&S today
With a baby in a chair: a little boy, I thought.
He (or she) had lost a shoe. I could not say
Whether left or right; it mattered to him (or her)
No more than it did to me. The shoe returned,
He promptly kicked it off again (if he was a he),
And then once more. I would have shouted,
Threatened, issued ultimata, scowled;
He, or she, would no doubt have howled,
Sensing in my panic a hostility,
A regret that fatherhood should so expose me
In a public place. The mother beautifully
Made a game of it: "Is it off again?
Shall we put it on. Oh look, again,
And shall we do it yet once more.?"
The child could only chuckle and, observing,
Share the joy of language as yet unlearnt,
Dimly perceiving, through it, love.

## April Rain

The rain felt new, fresh and cold
Falling on the old hills like a blessing,
Like a baptism betokening rebirth:
Streams ran down through the sloping woods,
Carrying twigs like swimming fish,
Cutting through the carpet of needles,
In black rivulets, thousands upon
Thousands, in a joyful breaking
Of the earth. The freezing drops
Cut into our cheeks, resolving
Themselves into hail, stirring
The stink of the earth: life
Born out of decomposition. I
Sang to have survived the winter,
And each note trembled in the rain
And fell to fragments in the wind.

## Two old ladies

Two old ladies, old and fat,
On octogenarian feet,
Arm linked to arm, one
Supporting, the other not;
Neither knowing which. Bag
Hanging like fruit from
The arm that dangles free.
They pay, why should they?
No heed to me.

Two old ladies, out for the day,
Not much to spend: time
Or money. Both are running low;
Husbands a memory,
Children gone, grandchildren
Indifferent , each other
For now to lean upon
And after, when one is gone,
A world to face alone.

# Rough Sleepers

In full daylight, under cloud,
The sun delayed, the rain
A rumour in the Bay of Biscay,
In the busy street, men sleep,
Between the vegan restaurants
And the Vietnamese,
Breathing in the fragances
Of exotic cuisines
They cannot afford to taste.
Men in urine -sodden blankets
Stinking of a hundred nights
Catching the reluctant warmth
Of noon. A few speak:
"Spare change?" No change
To spare in this town; we
Find coins, pressing into
A proffered hand, or dropped
Unto plastic cups that stand
Like inverted tulips. One
Man, legless and long-bearded,
Manages a grotesque jollity:
"Have a very lovely day," he calls
Out of God knows what unimagined
Hell. We pause, drop
A pound or two, retreat
Into our common guilt. This
Is now, and England, and yet
We bear it, and we forget.

## Growing

The clematis I planted last July
Is flowering now: green shoots
Steadying themselves on a fence
Of iron, purple heads nodding
To the wind. The indelicate spring
Is with us, ravaging from the west,
Bending flowers from which the colours drain
Bruising the daffodils with rain.
Life is once more importunate,
Breaking the soil, suffering the cold.
On the hills the lambs cavort away
Their twelve weeks of allotted life.
The world raises two fingers to entropy.
In the end, death always wins.

## Paying

Three checkouts had a computer screen,
The fourth, a human face, an accent
Like a Greenhalgh pie, a smile
And a hand for change, not a mouth
That vomits coinage on the floor.
She will soon, no doubt be gone
When the last human passes on
And emporia of vending machines
Serve a clientele of ants. But I
Turn to the old man in the queue
And say, "I like this not a lot".
The moment of quiet rebellion we share
Is pointless, satisfyingly doomed to fail.
But still, I pocket my pound coins
Hot from another human hand.

## Lost data

I sat down alone,
Forgotten my phone:
An idiot, a sap,
Forgotten my pacer app.
Nothing to be done later
Once you've lost the data.
Thousands of steps just gone;
None of them on the phone.
Miles I walked that day
And every inch just thrown away.
A debacle so complete
I might as well have lost my feet.

## Not playing the game

When I was a tiny boy,
I counted bits of coloured glass,
Round and blue and red and white,
Or pale with milky mist –
Possessed by capture in a sport
That really was a war.
But I, for shame
At my incompetence.
And fear that I would lose them all,
Never played the game.

Now that I am very old,
I count the days that pass
And those that I recall:
The days of joy, the days of shame,
The people that I loved,
And those that I betrayed;
Those there were I might have loved,
Who never knew, for I
Never played the game.

## Alesha's Death

I am old now, not much remaining,
Rich in memories that take the place
Of children, past for future. The cancer
Sleeps for now, but there is no grace
In my limbs, and the strength I had
Is fled. Soon I shall be dead.
But not so soon, I cannot glory
In the sunsets that remain, or weep
For murdered children. Who would kill
A child? Why would you murder life
At its source. Now, I have no choice
But to be gentle, no strength for strife,
No more capacity for rage, and yet
My weary, incontinent , ravaged age
Has not lost the gift of sorrow.
I weep, I weep and quietly hate
Those who murder tomorrow.

## Depression

I am back from holiday.
The sky, sympathetically, is grey.
Acting out for me
A pathetic fallacy.

And you are gone,
Leaving me alone,
Abandoning me
To enjoy my misery.

You will not be gone for long;
I shall listen to a doleful song,
While you are away,
Away on holiday.

# Nemi

A town haunts my imagination's eye,
Built of cypresses, old stone, blue sky.
We drank Frascati, ate strawberries and cream,
And wandered idly, as in a dream
Of far-off times, passed out of memory,
But fixed like spirochaeti in the artery
Where the blood runs reeking, hot and red;
And in the night the living call the dead
Forth from the dark heart of the lake.
The oleanders shiver, the pine branches break;
A hunted god runs, begging for a long-lost life
And a mad-eyed priest pursues with bloodied knife.
The swallows with scalpel wings dissect the air
And an old and frightful chaos is enacted there.

## No Worries

The waiter brought my chips and plaice.
"Thanks," I said, "No worries," he;
I was perplexed: who did he mean?
Himself? Or me? Or the fillets
Reclining on my plate. I felt
No such serenity, and the fish
Had gone beyond the aches
And itches of mortality. So he
Must be, perhaps for a moment,
Released from care; no anxiety;
No foreboding, no fear
Of poverty, old age, disease
Or death; hope exultant in his face,
And all from serving plaice.

# Trump

Melania Trump strides in her fuck-me shoes
Across the White House lawn. The most expensive
Rotavator in the world, and the loveliest. She sees
Ahead of her, hair lifted as if on a hinge,
By the waiting helicopter, the bulk that is
The Donald, leader of the land of the free
And friend of dictators everywhere. He stares
Into the misty distance, as becomes a visionary,
And his fleshy, Cola-bloated features assume the gloom
Of a fattened ox, invited to a hecatomb.

Melania Trump strides in her fuck-me shoes
Across the White House Lawn. A flag flies
At half mast. You think you hear a twittering
Of birds in the shrubbery; it is the whispering
Of indignant ghosts – of men and ideas,
Substantial once, now mere abstractions
Fit to fill a page of mindless rhetoric
Or feature in a presidential tweet.

## Final Test, Last Day

Again, the season ends in elegy,
As summers will. Elgar sounds
In the memory. Swallows
Punctuate the telephone wires
Like quavers on a stave. Soon,
They will be gone, and the white-clad
Young men; they too will be gone,
Gone south, beyond the blinding
Desert, or further still, into
The comfort of oblivion.

Old men love elegies; sentiment
Envelopes them in its sweet
And clinging fog. A summer gone,
A season ended, and still alive!
Only the white-shrouded winter
To survive; only the spring
To hope for, beyond the far hill,
Where the swallow glides, and will,
Though not for all, carry summer
On its dark and darting wing.

## Cat in the sun

The cat snared sunlight
Between his claws. The falling motes
Glittered in the air.

Beyond the window
The leaves clattered in the wind,
Breaking the silence.

A Japanese vase,
Chaste in its glowing stillness,
Fell to the tiled floor.

I saw it as it fell,
Waiting for its destruction,
My dissolution.

## Away

She has gone away
Away across the sky
And there is no home.

She may not return.
Life offers no guarantee;
Just one certainty.

The days are darker
As autumn overwhelms us
And the skies redden.

My mood is sombre,
As the light begins to dim
And she is not here.

## Visiting the Parthenon

We climbed the polished steps,
Holding a Baedeker,
Not a peplos; we pushed
Against a hoplite phalanx,
Bearing selfie-sticks, guided
By didactic women in quilted
Coats. Names flew past like
Late swallows: Kallikrates,
Ictinus, Pericles: but there
It still was, an eight-pronged
Trident threatening the sky,
Pulse-quickening; above,
A column-drum, hoisted
By a crane, wavered and found
A place first appointed
Twenty-five centuries before.

## Demented

I remember you not like this:
Staring-eyed and screaming,
Unwashed, unkempt, afraid,
Lost and alarmed in your silence,
Longing for the dark.

Where did you go, and when,
My ironic, gentle scholar,
Out of your world of books
And reminiscence and quiet
Evenings, shared with friends?

You walked with me the hills,
And levelled them with talk,
Stumbling on the Lakeland stones,
Half a mile into the sky,
Looking to a distant light,

And tracking through the cloud
The way ahead. With me
You watched the white-clad figures
Swoop like diving seabirds
On the pampered grass.

With me you traced the ebb
And flow of life along
The contours of a melody,
Hearts swelling to the sweet
Seduction of a song.

We loved the same woman,
Shared the same likes
And obscured our enmities
In the appeasing fog
Of easy humour.

And then, old age and loneliness
Broke and bewildered you.
You lost yourself and went
Somewhere I could not follow you
Or aspire to help.

And now, I do not know you:
Angry as you are, with a prophet's rage,
Wild-eyed, fanatic,
Revenant from the desert
And the unimaginable night.

## The Destroyer

I pity them, the innocent fools,
Arrayed in supermarket aisles,
Buying goods they will never use,
For seasons they will never see.

I pity them that do not know,
What I know, cannot see
What I see; that pass me by
And do not sense my power.

I see children who will never grow,
Old women who shortly will
No longer need their sticks
And trolleys or daughter's arms.

Shortly, I shall end them all:
The world and all that in it is,
The people and all the hopes
To which they foolishly aspire.

And this, like a God, I can do
Nonchalantly and without
Malevolence, with a closing
Of my eyes and a last rattling breath.

# Armistice Day

Rain, let there be rain;
There must be rain,
Lancashire rain
That softens the skein
And services the loom.

Not Flanders rain,
And not Gallipoli rain
That disinters the dead
And fills the trench
With woken ghosts.

Hymns, let there be hymns:
Hymns to summon,
Hymns to call and comfort:
Almighty father, strong to save,
Abide with me, my country.

A cenotaph
In a Lancashire town,
Facing a monument
To the mining dead,
Three hundred in a blink.

The names, the many names;
The roll-call going on
And no one answering,
The blood-red wreaths
On the wet stone floor.

One by one they came:
People and troops
Of people, institutions,
Societies, clubs, councils
Civic complexities.

All the bindweed
That grips the human dirt
And makes it solid:
Not a crowd; a commonwealth
Worth fighting for.

Worth dying for?
Who shall say.
It is Armistice Day
And those who have the right
Are buried far away.

Around us, the silence
Coalesces into grief;
Ahead of me, a dog, I swear
Senses the solemnity
And stands, silent, to attention.

## Goodbye to all that

In Amsterdam, the lights were on,
Reflected in the black canals, bright
Against the black walls of houses
Built for scoundrels. The bicycles
Were a silent menace, aimless
In the dark, thick as locusts. No one
Minded the meandering ghosts
That packed the streets, insubstantial
And ephemeral, lookers-on,
You and I and ten thousand others.

This, and then, and then no more:
Europe has been cancelled by Act
Of Parliament, and we that love it
Are found in treason, enemies
Of the people, citizens of nowhere.

## Love

I love you with all my years:
Those that are departed,
Those that are still to fear.
I love you with my old age
As I dreamed of you in youth.
I love you with my memories:
Those that still abide,
Those that have slipped away.
I love you with the strength I had
And the little I retain.
I love you will all my hopes:
Those that still remain
And when we lie, dissolute
In the dust, perhaps somewhere
There may reside a memory
Of the love that brought us there

# The Daily Round

I am a codger now. A coffin-dodger.
I wear an old git's uniform: pullover,
Pants I can't quite pull up; jacket
With a zip, as buttons have become
A challenge I cannot confront.

I wrap a muffler around my neck,
Thinner than it used to be, and wish
I had my thermals on. The ice
Keeps me a prisoner, only
The crossword for companion.

My cat is looking at me; he wants
My chair, my warm spot, the heat
Escaping from my body, of which
I am not aware, weakly
I surrender to his greater will.

The sun is out, and so I watch
The white edge of snow
For signs of melt, restless
And hoping to complete
The ten thousand steps I set myself.

Ten thousand, sometimes more:
But now I count steps, before,
I walked the heedless miles
On moor or mountain
And only counted larks.

I shall go to M and S
And sit awhile, and read
Until I feel the space I occupy
Is wanted for another. Then
I go, in search of purchases I do not want.

## Death too strong

I found the spider in the sink.
I might have flushed away
His black mass and steely legs.
Instead, I put a glass on him
And slipped a mat beneath.

And so, I bore him carefully
To the open window, and let
Him slide, down the surface
Of the glass, thinking that he might
Find himself outside.

He slid, and on the narrow sill
Crumpled, then was still.
Death had been too strong
For him, and so he lay,
Until the rain washed him away.

## Progress

All my life, I've been a looker -on
And hope no one would see
My idle curiosity.

I've never been a joiner-in,
Preferring not to be
Much in company.

And now, I am a clinger- on,
Hoping, helplessly,
Someone notices me.

Lightning Source UK Ltd.
Milton Keynes UK
UKHW011405150419
341049UK00001B/113/P